Places Along
the Way

By Brian Sargent

Subject Consultant
Chalice Bennett
Elementary Specialist
Martin Luther King Jr. Laboratory School
Evanston, Illinois

Reading Consultant
Cecilia Minden-Cupp, PhD
Former Director, Language and Literacy Program
Harvard Graduate School of Education

Children's Press®
A Division of Scholastic Inc.
New York   Toronto   London   Auckland   Sydney
Mexico City   New Delhi   Hong Kong
Danbury, Connecticut

Designer: Herman Adler
Photo Researcher: Caroline Anderson
The photo on the cover shows a girl getting ready to go on a trip.

Library of Congress Cataloging-in-Publication Data

Sargent, Brian, 1969–
   Places along the way / by Brian Sargent.
       p. cm. — (Rookie read-about math)
   Includes index.
   ISBN-10: 0-516-29917-4 (lib. bdg.)   0-531-16839-5 (pbk.)
   ISBN-13: 978-0-516-29917-4 (lib. bdg.)   978-0-531-16839-4 (pbk.)
   1. Place value (Mathematics)—Juvenile literature. 2. Numeration—Juvenile
literature. I. Title. II. Series.

   QA141.3.S37 2006
   513.5'5—dc22   2005032741

CHILDREN'S PRESS, and ROOKIE READ-ABOUT®,
and associated logos are trademarks and/or registered trademarks
of Scholastic Library Publishing. SCHOLASTIC and associated logos
are trademarks and/or registered trademarks of Scholastic Inc.

1 2 3 4 5 6 7 8 9 10 R 16 15 14 13 12 11 10 09 08 07

Today is an exciting day.
My family and I are going
to visit my grandma.

My grandma lives in Las Vegas. It is a long way from here. We will be in the car a long time.

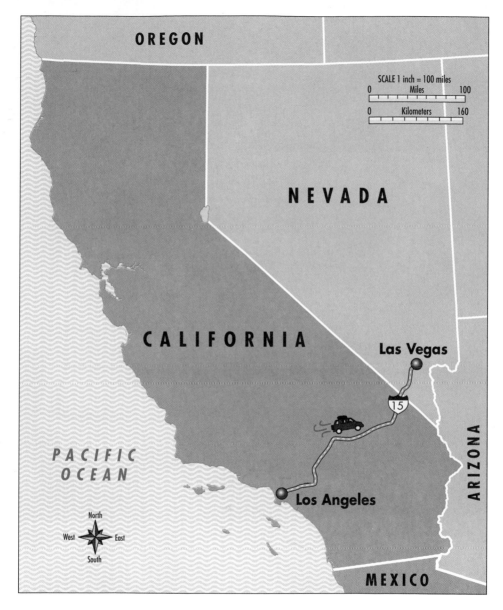

OREGON

NEVADA

CALIFORNIA

Las Vegas

15

Los Angeles

PACIFIC
OCEAN

ARIZONA

MEXICO

North
West · East
South

SCALE 1 inch = 100 miles
0   Miles   100
0   Kilometers   160

5

I won't get bored because
I know fun things to do in
the car. My favorite game
is called "Thousands,
Hundreds, Tens, and Ones."

This is how you play.
You look for signs with
numbers. The bigger the
number, the better.

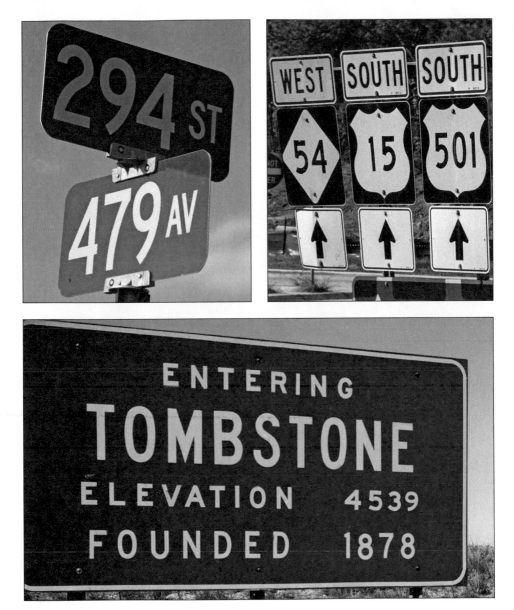

10

When you are in a city, you can find numbers on street signs or houses. This sign has the number 7300. That's 7 thousands, 3 hundreds, with no tens or ones.

Here's how I mark that on my paper. I put a 7 under "Thousands" and a 3 under "Hundreds." Since there are no tens or ones, I put a 0 under "Tens" and a 0 under "Ones."

thousands	hundreds	tens	ones
7	3	0	0

13

Now we're on the highway. The speed limit is 65 miles per hour. I know that 65 means 6 tens and 5 ones.

This is how I write that number on my paper. I put a 6 under "Tens" and a 5 under "Ones."

Here's the highway to Las Vegas. The sign says 15. That is 1 ten and 5 ones. I'll write that down, too. Where would I put the 1 and the 5?

Let's look for more signs. I see the number 533 on that exit sign. That means 5 hundreds, 3 tens, and 3 ones. I'll put that on my paper.

21

There is a curve ahead.
We need to slow down
to 30 miles per hour.
I'll write down 3 tens
and no ones.

We are going through a town. Look at the number on this sign! There are 825 people living here.

thousands	hundreds	tens	ones
7	3	0	0
		6	5
		1	5
	5	3	3
		3	0
	8	2	5

The number 825 will be the last one on my chart. It has 8 hundreds, 2 tens, and 5 ones. I'm done!

Welcome to Las Vegas. We'll be at Grandma's house soon. I can't wait to tell her about my number game. What a fun trip!

29

Words You Know

curve   exit

highway

hundreds

ones

tens

thousands

Index

About the Author

Brian Sargent is a middle school math teacher. He lives in Glen Ridge, New Jersey, with his wife, Sharon, and daughters, Kathryn, Lila, and Victoria. His grandma does not live in Las Vegas.

Photo Credits

Photographs © 2007: Corbis Images: 29 (B.S.P.I.), 25 (Gary Braasch), 18, 30 bottom (David Butow/SABA), 22, 30 top left (Klaus Hackenberg/zefa), 10 (Robert Landau), 21, 30 top right (Joseph Sohm; ChromoSohm Inc.); Folio, Inc.: 9 top left (Everett C. Johnson), 9 top right (Tom McCarthy); Index Stock Imagery/Gary Connor: 14; Richard Hutchings Photography: cover, 3, 6, 13, 17, 26, 31; TRIP Photo Library/Earl Young: 9 bottom.

Map by Bob Italiano